SIMPLE
SLOPES

ANDREW DUNN

**Illustrated by
ED CARR**

Thomson Learning

New York

Titles in this series
Heat
It's Electric
Lifting by Levers
The Power of Pressure
Simple Slopes
Wheels at Work

First published in the
United States in 1993 by
Thomson Learning
115 Fifth Avenue
New York, NY 10003

First published in 1991 by
Wayland Publishers Ltd.

Copyright © 1991 Wayland Publishers Ltd.

U.S.version copyright © 1993 Thomson Learning

Cataloging-in-Publication Data applied for

ISBN 1-56847-017-7

Printed in Italy

Contents

Words in *italic* are explained in the glossary on page 30.

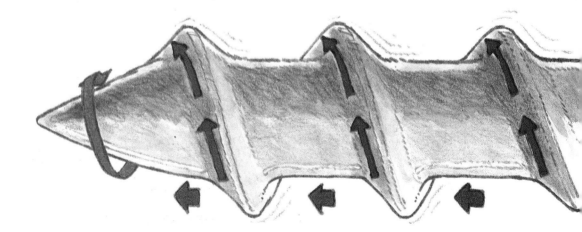

Getting to the top

Have you ever climbed a mountain or walked up a hill? If you have, you know that the steeper the slope, the harder it is to walk up it. This has nothing to do with your legs or how healthy you are. It is a law of nature.

Raising an object (like you) by a certain distance (to the top of a hill) takes a fixed amount of work, or energy, no matter how you do it. Since work is the product of force and distance (Force x Distance = Work),

you can make any task easier by changing the way you do it.

You can do the same amount of work, using the same amount of energy, by using either a lot of effort over a short distance or a little effort over a long distance. The steepest route is shortest and hardest. A gentle slope is easier but longer. Either way, you will have done the same amount of work by the time you reach the top.

On this steep mountainside, walkers have made a zigzag path by walking across the slope instead of straight up it. It is longer, but it is much easier.

What is work?

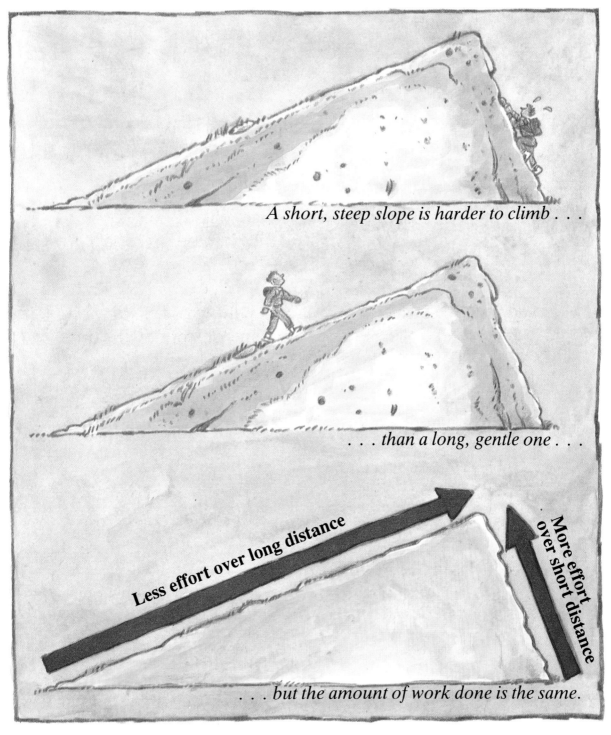

A short, steep slope is harder to climb . . .

. . . than a long, gentle one . . .

Less effort over long distance

More effort over short distance

. . . but the amount of work done is the same.

Lifting loads

The simplest way to lift a heavy object is to haul it straight up. However, this is not the easiest way, because it takes the most effort.

In the picture below, the *ramp* is three times as long as the height of the wall. So it takes only a third of the effort to lift the load to the same height. The person is using less effort over a longer distance.

The ramp is one of the oldest *machines* there is. The ancient Egyptians used ramps to build their *pyramids*. They had no *cranes*, so to raise the enormous blocks of stone, they used ramps. You can still see ramps on building sites today.

Today people use the ramp—a simple slope—in all sorts of ways. There are ramps in everything from plows to zippers, from keys and locks to screws, nuts, and bolts.

How to build a pyramid

Wedges

A very useful type of slope is the wedge. It appears in many machines in different forms. It can even be a machine by itself —a door wedge is an example.

When you use a door wedge, instead of moving an object up the slope, the slope moves to lift the object. As the wedge is pushed under the door, it raises the door slightly with a lot of force. The door presses back down on the wedge with *equal* force, so that the wedge grips the floor firmly and holds the door open.

Slope moves under door.

Moving slope raises door.

Door presses down with equal force.

Arches

Another example of a wedge is the stone used at the top of an arch. It is called the keystone, and it presses on both sides of the arch, forcing the other stones together and giving the arch great strength.

The next time you see an arch like this, look carefully for a wedge-shaped stone at the top.

Cutting wedges

An ax is a wedge that has a sharp edge and is attached to a handle.

A wedge is really made up of two slopes back to back. When an ax strikes a log, the moving slope on each side pushes the wood away sideways, splitting it in two. The effort is *magnified* by the length of the slopes.

Most machines that people cut things with—scissors, shears, can openers, hedge trimmers— involve wedges.

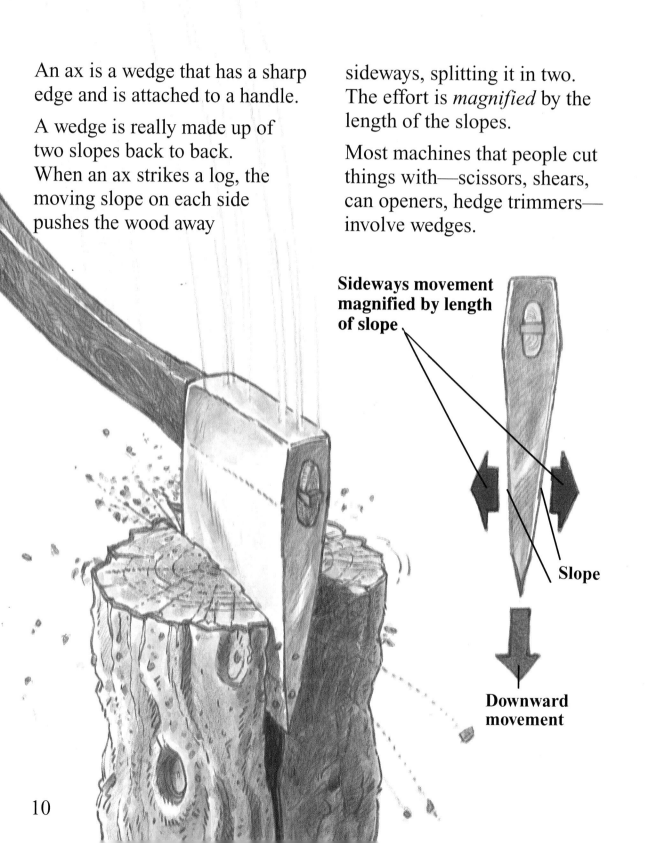

Sideways movement magnified by length of slope

Slope

Downward movement

Scissors

Scissors are made of two wedges that cut through cloth or paper by slicing into it from opposite directions. As the *blades* meet, they act like one wedge, forcing the material to part sideways. Garden shears work in exactly the same way.

Hedge trimmers

An electric hedge trimmer uses two blades that slide backward and forward over each other. Each blade has many slots, and each has a sharp wedge shape.

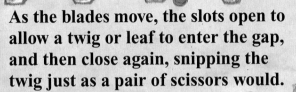

As the blades move, the slots open to allow a twig or leaf to enter the gap, and then close again, snipping the twig just as a pair of scissors would.

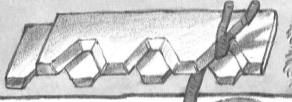

So using a hedge trimmer is like using dozens of pairs of scissors very close together, all at the same time.

The plow

The plowman's wedge

When farmers plow their fields, they cut into the top of the soil, lift it, and turn it over. This breaks up the soil and mixes some air and old plants with it. It is then ready to have a new crop planted in it. A plow is a set of wedges dragged through the soil by a tractor, a horse, or an ox. It has been used by farmers for thousands of years. The only difference is that today it is made of metal instead of wood.

A plow is in fact made of three wedges. The first one cuts a slice down through the soil.

First wedge

The second cuts sideways into the soil under the surface, separating a layer of earth.

Second wedge

The third lifts this layer and turns it over. All the wedges produce big forces as they are dragged through the soil.

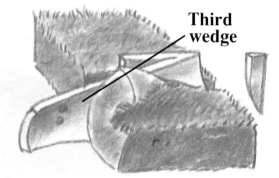

Third wedge

Modern plows work in exactly the same way as the ones used by farmers thousands of years ago. Can you see the wedges cutting through the soil?

The zipper

The zipper is a clever *device* that changes the small effort of pulling on it into a strong force that either pushes tiny teeth together or separates them. Each tooth slots into the one above it.

In the middle of the zipper is a wedge. If you have ever had a stuck zipper, you know that if the wedge is not between the teeth of the zipper it is very difficult to separate them.

When you close the zipper again, the two outer sides of the zipper also act as wedges and push the teeth back into place.

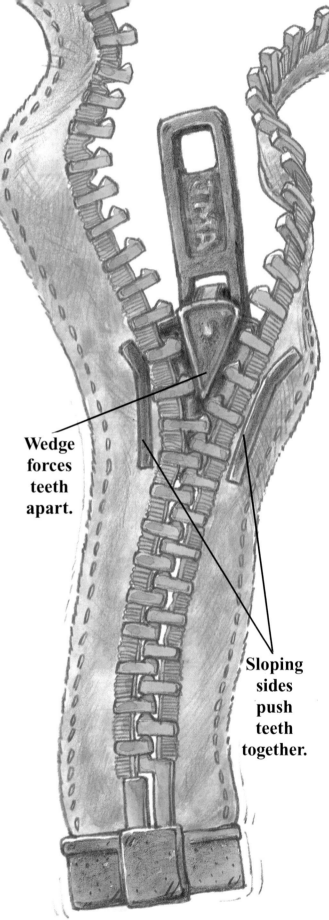

Wedge forces teeth apart.

Sloping sides push teeth together.

The zipper was invented in 1891 for fastening boots.

14

The wedge in nature

The wedge appears
in nature as a very
powerful tool.

If a crack
appears in rock,
rainwater will
seep into it.

During the winter
when the water freezes,
it *expands* as it
turns into ice. The
sideways force is
strong enough
to break the rock.

This is what causes
roads to break up in
winter and *boulders*
to break away
from cliffs.

The key in the lock

Many machines use the principle of slopes without using wedges. Have you ever looked carefully at the key to a door? If you have, you know that it is not easy to see how it works, because you also need to look inside the lock!

Cylinder locks

In a *cylinder* lock, the barrel (cylinder) is held by pins. The pins are pushed through holes in the barrel by strong springs so that the barrel cannot turn.

Locked: Pins keep the barrel from turning.

Each pin has two parts, one above the other, which are not connected. If each pin is raised so that the gaps between the parts line up, the barrel is free to turn and the lock can be opened.

Locked: Ramp raises pins the wrong amount.

But the gap in each pin is at a different point, so each has to be raised by a different amount.

The answer is to make a key that has a different sloping ramp for each pin. As the key is slipped into the lock, each ramp pushes up the pins until the key is in the correct position to raise all the pins the right amount.

Of course, the key has to slip out of the lock as well, so in between each ramp is another ramp facing the opposite way.

When the correct key is in the lock, the barrel can turn and pull back the bolt to unlock the door.

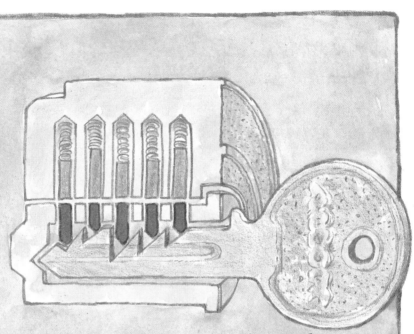

Unlocked: Five ramps raise the pins the correct amount, but the key is stuck.

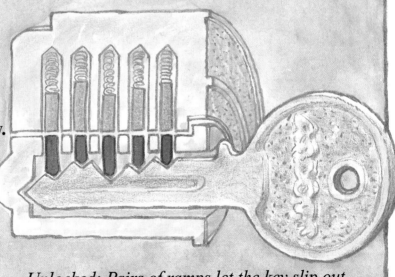

Unlocked: Pairs of ramps let the key slip out.

17

The screw

Take a look at a screw. Can you see the slope? A screw is made up of a long slope cut around and around a metal rod. The slope works in the same way as it does in a ramp. Because of the length of the slope, it produces great force with little effort.

When you drive a screw into a block of wood, the screw itself travels only a short distance. But as it turns, the slope around it travels much farther, magnifying the effort of turning and driving the screw powerfully forward. After a few turns, the screw is held firmly in place.

A corkscrew slide lets you travel far in a short distance—just like the slope of a screw does.

Screw travels short distance with great force

Slope travels long distance

Small turning effort

Nuts and bolts

Nuts and bolts work in the same way as screws.

A nut has to turn around the bolt many times to travel a short distance along it. The force needed to turn it is very low, because the slope is very long and gentle.

But because the nut moves along the bolt very slowly, the force it produces is very great. This powerful grip is what makes nuts and bolts hold objects together so tightly.

Screws at work

Corkscrews

A corkscrew is a pointed *spiral* of metal that works just like a wood screw. It can be screwed into the cork easily, and it grips the cork tightly.

Jacks

A jack is used for lifting a car easily off the ground to change a tire. The screw has to turn many times to lift the car a few inches. If the handle moves around fifty times as far as the car moves up, then it is fifty times easier to lift the car than it would be without the jack.

Looking at faucets

Try this experiment. Turn on the kitchen faucet and then try to stop the water by using your finger. Be careful, or you will soak yourself and the kitchen!

Do you see what enormous *pressure* the water has? Yet a faucet can stop the water easily.

The effort of your hand is first magnified by the handle, which acts as a *lever*. Inside the faucet there is a screw, which forces the *washer* down into the hole with great force.

The screw has a steeply sloping thread so that it does not take many turns to close or open the faucet.

Archimedes' and other screws

One of the earliest uses of the screw as a machine was by Archimedes. He was a mathematician who lived in ancient Greece more than two thousand years ago. He made a machine to lift water out of the *hold* of a ship.

He put a spiral slope inside a watertight cylinder. As the handle was turned, the screw lifted the water up the spiral.

Archimedes' screw is still used in some parts of the world to help water crops.

These farmers are using a version of Archimedes' screw to raise water from a stream to their fields.

Augers

Today you are more likely to see the principle of Archimedes' screw at work in machines called *augers*. These are used, for example, on modern building sites. They make deep holes in the ground for the *foundation columns* of tall buildings.

An auger is like a large screw. As it turns in the ground, it lifts the soil up its spiral slope.

When it is full, it is lifted up to the surface and emptied. Then it can be lowered again for another load.

Other augers

This auger is being used to drill holes for the foundations of a new building.

Augers are used in tunneling through soil and rocks. In a machine called a tunnel mole, cutting blades scrape away at the soil or rock face as they turn. Behind them, an auger moves the scrapings away from the cutting blades.

Meat Grinders

You can find an auger in a butcher's shop if the shop has an old-fashioned meat grinder.

The meat grinder handle turns both an auger and the cutting blades. The auger moves the meat forward, forcing it past the blades that grind it and then out through the holes in the front.

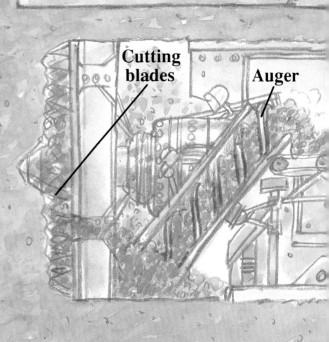

Cutting blades

Auger

Cutting plates

Auger

The handle
is also a lever, which
magnifies the effort
of turning it. Together,
the lever and the auger
produce an enomous
force on the meat.

Conveyer belt

Waste cart

25

Drills

Drills are similar to augers, because they use the slope of the screw to carry material away. If the material stayed in the hole as it was drilled, the *drill bit* would quickly jam solid and stick fast. So, as the drill cuts forward with its sharp point, the waste is carried away backward along the screw of the drill.

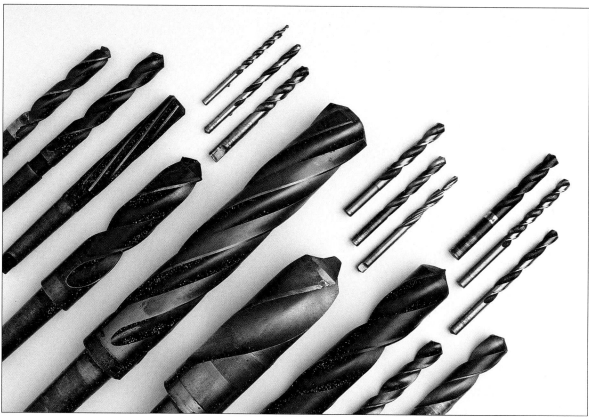

Drill bits come in many sizes. It is important to use the right one for the job.

In big drills, the grooves are deep and the slopes very gentle.

Have you ever seen metal being drilled? The waste that comes out has been bent around the drill bit, so it often has a corkscrew shape, like a pig's tail.

In fine drills, the grooves are very shallow and the slopes very steep.

27

The simplicity of slopes

At first sight, the simple slope, or the inclined plane as engineers call it, looks too simple to be a useful machine. Yet even a wedge can be a very powerful tool. Many machines operate on extremely simple principles. Even the most complicated machines, including ones that are full of electronics, are often based on very simple ideas.

The bow of a ship is like a huge wedge that cuts easily through the water.

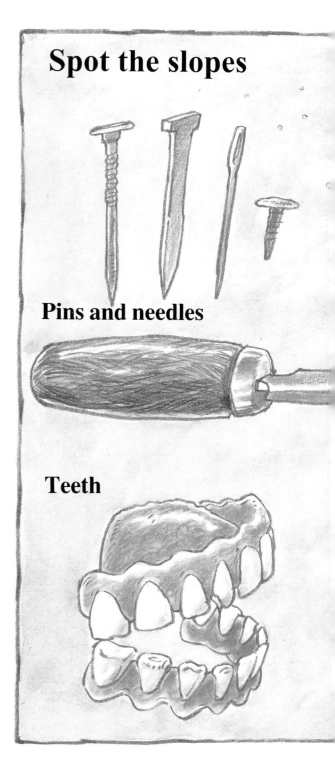

Spot the slopes

Pins and needles

Teeth

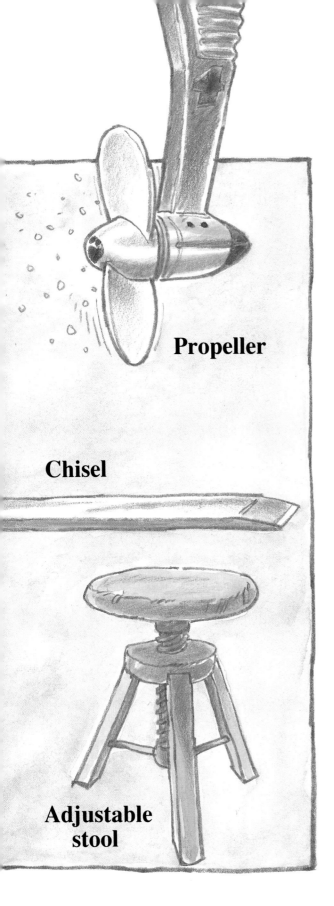

Propeller

Chisel

Adjustable stool

Propellers have sloping blades that "throw" the air backward, making the aircraft move forward.

The next time you use a tool or machine, ride in one, or see one at work in the street or on television, see if you can find the simple idea that is the basis of it. You will be surprised by how often you can!

Glossary

Augers   Pieces of machinery shaped like screws; often used for drilling holes in the ground.

Blades   Sharp cutting edges, found, for example, on knives, scissors, or lawnmowers.

Boulder   A very large rock.

Cranes   Tall towers with long arms at the top; used on building sites.

Cylinder   A round tube. Cylinders can be solid or hollow.

Device   A small machine or an especially intricate one.

Drill bit   The part of a drill that does the cutting.

Equal   The same amount or the same force in two or more things.

Expand   To grow bigger.

Foundation columns   Deep, round pillars of strong concrete sunk into the ground to provide a solid base for large buildings.

Hold   The part of a ship where the cargo is stored.

Lever   A bar that balances or turns on a point called a fulcrum. By using a small force to move one end of the bar a long distance, you can produce a bigger force at the other end. Like a slope, a lever is a simple machine.

Machines   A machine is anything made by people to make work easier to do.

Magnified   Made bigger or greater.

Pressure   The amount of force with which something presses on something else.

Pyramids   The large buildings that the ancient Egyptians made to hold the body of a dead king or queen. A pyramid has triangular sides that meet in a point at the top.

Ramp   A smooth human-made slope between places of different heights.

Spiral   A shape like a coil.

Washer   A flat rubber ring used in a water faucet. When the faucet is closed the washer is pushed down tightly to keep any water from dripping out. When open, it is raised to let water flow.

Books to read

For younger readers:

How Machines Work by Christopher Rawson
(EDC Publishing, 1976)
How Things Work by Robin Kerrod
(Marshall Cavendish, 1970)
Simple Machines by Rae Bains
(Troll, 1985)

For older readers:

Archimedes: Greatest Scientist of the Ancient World by D. C. Ipsen
(Enslow, 1988)
Pyramid by David Macaulay
(Houghton Mifflin, 1975)
The Random House Book of How Things Work by Steve Parker
(Random House, 1991)
The Way Things Work by David Macaulay
(Houghton Mifflin, 1988)

Picture acknowledgments

The publishers would like to thank the following for providing the photographs for this book: Cephas Picture Library 24 (Nigel Blythe), 29 (D. Burrows); Chapel Studios 18, 26; Frank Lane Picture Agency 13 (Maurice Walker); G.S.F. Picture Library 22; PHOTRI 28; Science Photo Library 14 (John Heseltine); Tony Stone Worldwide 4.

Index